HOSTADANCE

WRITTEN AND PHOTOGRAPHED BY

ROBERT J. ZIMMER

A SPECIAL THANK YOU TO ALL OF THE DESIGNERS AND GARDENERS WHO ALLOWED ME TO PHOTOGRAPH THEIR PASSION, AS WELL AS TO SILVER MIST GARDEN CENTER, ROSE-HILL GARDENS, GRAZIANO GARDENS, LAND OF THE GIANTS HOSTA FARM, PONDSIDE GARDENS, THE HOSTA STOP AND THE GREEN BAY BOTANICAL GARDEN.

ELEMENTS OF THE DANCE

The wonder and glory of hostas

Hostadance

Just as exciting and interesting to me over the past few years as growing massive specimen hostas in the garden has been experimenting with using hostas in containers of all types.

While this may not be the traditional way to grow and garden with hostas, growing these plants in containers and combining them with an assortment of other garden treasures opens up the world of hostas to a whole new audience of potential hosta fans.

This book is not a horticulture lesson in hostas, nor is it a technical hosta growing manual. There are plenty of those on the market. My book is a gallery of gardening ideas and inspiration using my favorite plant.

One of the biggest trends in gardening, noted by many professionals in the industry, is the move away from classifying plants as annual or perennial. The new generation of "yard decorators," are not as interested in whether a plant is annual or perennial. They are simply looking for a plant they love. A plant they are drawn to and attracted to.

To gain new followers and new fans, we must present hostas as more than simply landscape specimens and turn the eyes of this new generation of gardeners toward these exceptional plants that are elegantly showcased in containers and planters throughout the seasons.

These gardeners are also notably impatient. Patience is a trait is that is especially desirable when nurturing slow growing hostas to perfect maturity. Instant gratification and instant impact is more important to many of these new gardeners than the timeless and patient journey of observing your hostas as they build to sheer perfection.

I have especially enjoyed combining hostas with flowering annuals, ornamental grasses, as well as perennials and foliage plants to create breathtaking container and patio planter combinations.

Hostas do especially well in containers, even hanging baskets, with little care required. They benefit nicely from the additional water required for flowering annuals, and their colors, form and textures work wonderfully with plants of all types.

Their versatility and durability, as well as their elegant growth form and long lasting beauty make hostas the perfect choice for containers and planters.

Hostadance is a celebration of gardening with hostas and spectacular companion plants in ways that will surprise and delight. A seamless blend of hosta passion and a love for other garden treasures, such as annuals, perennials, bulbs, grasses and more, you'll discover a wealth of inspiration dancing across the coming pages.

Hostas, more than perhaps any other garden plants, captivate and thrill those who nurture their breathtaking form.

Hostadance will showcase that beloved experience on a whole new stage.

Let the Hostadance commence.

H. Golden Meadows

H. Dawn's Early Light

H. Lakeside Reflecting Glass

An Ocean of Blue...

H. Deep Blue Sea & First Frost

H. Lakeside Symphony

H. Irish Luck

H. Lakeside Paisley Print

H. Risky Business

Heirlooms and memories...

Awakening

H. Abiqua Drinking Gourd

H. Guardian Angel & friends

GARDEN INSPIRATION

Dancing in the shadows

The hosta dance commences as the first warm breath of spring billows across the garden, thawing our precious soils, and souls, as our treasured lovelies peek through to introduce themselves to their companions for the spring ball.

Creating combinations of glory, beauty and wonder is a passion of many gardeners, who will go to great lengths to bring to life their floral and foliage palette. Hostas make poetic companion plants for a number of other garden treasures, mingling seamlessly in harmony and exuding a melody all their own.

Throughout the four seasons, a tapestry of colors and textures sweeps through the garden in waves, designed with long-lasting, ever changing beauty, interest and curiosity in mind.

Experiment with a variety of perennials, annuals, ornamental grasses, trees, shrubs and bulbs to truly embrace the dance.

Do not, however, feel pressured to try too hard. Often times, the most interesting and exquisite designs are those that have been simply borne out of chance. As Mother Nature works her magic in the garden, you are sure to discover joyful wonders as plants pop up where they were never intended, but fit with perfection.

Or, you may find unexpected beauty in random plantings that suddenly blend together in heavenly unison.

Taking advantage of the texture, colors, growth forms, blooms and foliage of hosta dance partners is an endless journey of happiness and rebirth, discovery and joy, a satisfying reward to the soul as the beauty and elegance of your garden creations take form and come to life.

HERE ARE SOME OF MY FAVORITE PERENNIAL PARTNERS FOR HOSTAS IN THE GARDEN:

Coral bells *(Huechera sp.)*

Ornamental grasses *(var.)*

Maidenhair fern *(Adiantum)*

Trillium *(Tillium)*

Foamflower *(Tiarella)*

Jacob's Ladder *(Polmonium)*

Chocolate Joe-pye weed *(Eupatorium)*

Astilbe *(Astilbe)*

Creeping Jenny (*Lysimachia*)

Aralia (*Aralia*)

Roger's flower (*Rodgersia*)

Toad lily (*Tricyrtis*)

Ligularia (*Ligularia*)

Daylily (*Hemercallis*)

Lilium (*Lilium*)

Hellebores (*Helleborus*)

Columbine (*Aquilegia*)

Lady's Mantle (*Alchemilla*)

Mayapple (*Podophyllum*)

Jack-in-the-pulpit (*Arisaema*)

Wild Ginger (*Asarum*)

Monkshood (*Aconitum*)

Wild blue phlox (*Phlox*)

Allium (*Allium*)

Painter's Palette (*Persicaria*)

Cardinal flower (*Lobelia*)

Martagon Lily (*Lilium*)

Lady slipper (*Cypripedium*)

Virginia Bluebells (*Mertensia*)

Primrose (*Primula*)

Japanese Painted fern (*Athyrium*)

Peony (*Paeonia*)

Garden of Betty Humphrey

SOME OF MY FAVORITE ANNUALS TO USE IN HOSTA COMBINATIONS:

Coleus (*Coleus*)

Ornamental grasses (*var.*)

Super bells (*Calibrachoa*)

Petunia (*Petunia*)

Lantana (*Lantana*)

Calla (*Calla*)

Persian Shield (*Strobilanthes*)

Nemesia (*Nemesia*)

Creeping Jenny (*Lysimachia*)

Begonia (*Begonia*)

Impatiens (*Impatiens*)

Boston fern (*Nephrolepis*)

Asparagus fern (*Asparagus*)

Confetti fern (*Pilea*)

Ornamental pepper (*Capsicum*)

Icicle Licorice plant *(Helichrysum)*

Licorice plant *(Helichrysum)*

Wire vine *(Muehlenbeckia)*

Geranium *(Pelargonium)*

Alyssum *(Lobularia)*

Fuchsia *(Fuchsia)*

Sweet potato vine *(Ipomoea)*

Here, a stunning specimen of H. Liberty is surrounded by a ring of lush H. Golden Tiara.

Garden of Betty Humphrey

Garden of Sally Marchel Handrich

A standout hosta border features H. Great Expectations as its anchor, sweeping the full length of the lush landscape, shadowed by towering shagbark hickory and conifers.

Garden of Betty Humphrey

Coral Bells (Heuchera sp.) are some of the most popular hosta companion plants, available in a wide range of sizes, foliage and flower colors. Easy to grow and compact, these plants provide color and texture with their feathery bloom spikes.

Separated by a river of rich purple coral bells, H. Gunther's Prize and H. Beckoning anchor this breathtaking setting.

Unexpected companions in the garden, Carex Toffee Twist, along with bronze coral bell surround the brilliance of H. Patriot's Fire.

Garden of Audrey Temmer

$\mathcal{B}$lack Lace Elderberry *(Sambucus)* with its breathtaking feathery foliage in rich, deep purple and pale pink flower clusters, sprawls wildly among hostas in the garden of Audrey Temmer.

Garden of Audrey Temmer

Garden of Audrey Temmer

A lacy umbrella of deep, dark foliage shadows giant H. Solar Flare, providing a full three seasons of beauty in the garden.

Garden of Audrey Temmer

The elegance and texture of many Japanese and Korean maples (*Acer*) make ideal hosta companions. Here, H. Bridal Falls is touched by grace.

Garden of Sally Marchel Handrich

Garden of Audrey Temmer

Many variegated and pagoda dogwood (*Cornus*) selections grow well in shade to part sun and provide superb beauty and structure as they flow above a seas of hostas.

King Shade Garden at the Green Bay Botanical Garden

Golden Shadows pagoda dogwood, with its layered form and striking variegate foliage in green and gold, is the perfect companion for giant H. Blue Angel.

Garden of Carl and Karen Vanden Heuvel

*B*leeding heart Gold Heart (*Dicentra or Lamprocapnos*) with its brilliant golden yellow foliage and rich, pink and white blooms, flowers for several weeks in spring, its delicate texture and contrasting colors providing the perfect backdrop here for H. Spacious Skies.

Garden of Audrey Temmer

Garden of Betty Humphrey

The candelabra blooms of Japanese primrose *(Primula)*, along with dwarf goatsbeard *(Aruncus)* and a seedling golden coral bell *(Heuchera)* naturalize themselves around the misted beauty of H. Guardian Angel.

King Shade Garden at the Green Bay Botanical Garden

Coleus in blood red provides an unforgettable backdrop to the feathered beauty of H. Liberty in fun sun. Many newer coleus varieties are sun tolerant, making them even more versatile in the garden.

King Shade Garden at the Green Bay Botanical Garden

A pleasant and unexpected surprise, gardener Audrey Temmer was delighted when this purple variety of cushion spurge *(Euphorbia)* emerged and spread its delicate foliage over and among the chameleon-like leaves of H. Winfield Mist.

Garden of Audrey Temmer

The rich, deep blue of H. Hot Cakes dances with the feathery fronds of this silvery green tattered fern.

Garden of Audrey Temmer

Garden of Sally Marchel Handrich

*J*apanese painted fern (*Athyrium*) is a no-fail hosta companion wherever it is included in the garden. Here, the dance continues with H. Marilyn Monroe and H. Nigrescens.

The icy beauty of this variegated carex sedge completes an inspiring trio featuring Japanese painted fern and H. Brave Amherst.

Garden of Betty Humphrey

Garden of Betty Humphrey

Garden of Sally Marchel Handrich

Ferns, in general, are the perfect companions for hostas in the garden, providing rich texture, vertical interest and wild beauty as they dance among our treasured masterpiece specimens.

Garden of Sally Marchel Handrich

Sometimes, the mysterious appearance of pop-up plants in the garden offers the most unexpected and wonderful rewards. In this garden, orange milkweed, or butterfly weed (*Asclepias*), suddenly appeared, flanked by giant H. Climax.

Garden of Sally Marchel Handrich

Succulents and miniature hostas dance together in this delightful, explosive trio.

Spring and early summer blooming orchids, such as this Showy Lady slipper, are highly prized shade companion plants for hosta gardeners.

Garden of Audrey Temmer

One of my favorite trees for shady spots is the striking Tri-Color Beech (*Fagus*), with foliage that emerges green, silver and pink, growing more intense throughout the season.

Garden of Jerry Borlen

Old-fashioned Annabelle hydrangea form a lovely wall of beauty as they bloom throughout summer and fall around this fantastic specimen of H. Gunther's Prize.

Ornamental onion, or Allium, are fall-planted bulbs that bloom during May and June, providing unusual beauty with their spherical blooms in shades of purple, lavender, blue and white.

*J*apanese species lily Uchida, with richly spotted blooms in pink, red and white, is a fall-blooming lily that provides late season beauty in the shade garden.

Spring blooming bulbs, such as these multi-flowering daffodils are perfect companions for massive hostas like H. Gentle Giant, seen here as it begins to unfurl among a sea of gold.

King Shade Garden at the Green Bay Botanical Garden

Garden of Betty Humphrey

The cascading form of Japanese forest grass (*Hakonechloa*) never fails to provide captivating texture and flowing beauty in the shade garden, especially when allowed to tumble naturally over rocks and ledges.

Colorful geraniums capture the eye while H. Sagae, H. Foxfire Off Limits and H. June surround the colorful blooms and golden sedge.

Garden of Audrey Tenmer

$\mathcal{G}$olden grasses and sedges are wonderful companion plants for shady locations, here with wonderfully corrugated H. Brother Stefan.

SOLO INSPIRATIONS

The magic of hostas in Containers

To place a hosta in the confines of an elaborate container is to give the plant a whole new outlook on life. Even the most common, overlooked, older hostas in the garden come to exciting and vibrant new life when displayed prominently in a container.

Choosing the right container is as much a part of the process as planting your prized specimen. Containers in colors and textures that match or contrast the chosen prize are ideal.

Overwintering hostas in containers is relatively simple, at least here in my Zone 5 garden. I, along with many of the designers in this book, overwinter plants by simply moving them to an unheated garage, shed or outbuilding. A few gardeners will over winter their container hostas by removing them from the pot and temporarily placing them in the garden or in a trench for the winter season.

Another option that has been successful for a few friends who showcase container hostas is to simply bury the hosta, pot and all, into their backyard compost pile.

Hostas with a vase-shaped form, or those with cascading leaves work exceptionally well as container plants. Miniatures, as well as those with striking variegation or streaking, also work well as container specimens in the garden.

Be sure to water well, since container hostas will require more moisture than those situated in garden beds.

Select a few of your favorites this year and you'll never look at growing hostas the same way again.

H. Snake Eyes

Design by Tammy Borden

Courtesy of Conny Parsons

H. Curly Fries

Design by Audrey Temmer

H. Grand Tiara

Design by Leslie Kerk

H. Wide Brim

Design by Gardens of the Fox Cities

Design by Tammy Borden

H. Monkey Business

Design by Tammy Borden

H. Praying Hands

Design by Audrey Temmer

*A*n assortment of single specimen hosta containers is the perfect option where tree roots or rocks prevent in-ground planting.

Courtesy of Conny Parsons

Design by Gladys and Herb King

Design by Tammy Borden

Courtesy of Conny Parsons

H. B;ue Flame & H. Striptease

Courtesy of Conny Parsons

H. Sharp Dressed Man

Design by Patricia Gwidt

Design by Patricia Gwidt

Courtesy of Conny Parsons

*A*n adorable cat and mouse display featuring H. Dancing Mouse with concrete cat planter and friend.

Design by Sally Marchel Handrich

H. Christmas Tree

Design by Tammy Borden

Design by Tammy Borden

Courtesy of Conny Parsons

ENSEMBLE

A New Frontier in Fantasy Container Creations

*N*ow that you've successfully experimented with growing hostas in containers, it is time to take the next step - combining your favorite hosta treasures with annuals, perennials, ornamental grasses and more to create fantasy container combinations that will leave garden visitors breathless.

Take advantage of the wonderful textures, colors and forms of your favorite hostas and pair them with a variety of other container plants. You'll enjoy the thrilling results.

Some of my favorite container partners for hostas are ornamental grasses, ferns and annuals, such as coleus, lantana and begonias.

As in container gardening as a whole, try to incorporate plants that fit three growing styles. First, include a centerpiece plant, or a "thriller." This may be your hosta, but not necessarily.

Next comes your "filler." These are the plants that form the bulk of the container. In many cases, this may be your hosta specimen.

The third and type of plant to include in your container is your "spiller," those plants that cascade over the edge of the pot in a graceful, elegant manner. Once again, in certain cases, this may be your hosta. It may also be annual vines, annual flowers, or foliage plants such as ivy, creeping Jenny or coleus.

Select plants that provide contrasting colors, textures and form when creating your container masterpieces.

On the following pages, you'll discover tantalizing examples of container combinations featuring beloved hostas to inspire your new hobby.

Enjoy the Hostadance.

*I*n this combination set in a tall, pillar container, Mexican feather grass *(Nassella)*, lavender *(Lavandula)*, English ivy *(Hedera)*, Irish moss *(Chondrus)* and H. Stained Glass form an elegant display.

Design by Erica Smith

Courtesy of Conny Parsons

98

I love everything about H. Monkey Business, from its deep red stems to gently rippling, cascading leaves and bright gold edge.

Design by Audrey Temmer

*I*n shade, the rich turquoise of H. Krossa Regal dances with a variegated sedge and richly veined coral bell *(Heuchera)*.

Design by Rob Zimmer

In a sunny, bright pot, H. Liberty sprawls wide over a pillow of yellow begonias while a sprig of Sedum Angelina cascades over the rim. Alongside the container, the rich, deep blackish purple of companion coral bells adds spectacular drama.

Design by Betty Humphrey

With sunset colored stones adding wonderful texture and color, H. Rhino Hide joins Creeping Jenny *(Lysimachia)* and Joseph's Coat *(Alternanthera)*, along with trailing Wandering Jew *(Tradescantia)* in a perfect setting.

Design by Rob Zimmer

Design by Rob Zimmer

The misted perfection of H. Guardian Angel meets the golden glory of Japanese Forest Grass All Gold *(Hakonechloa)* in a towering yellow container. This grass is heavenly for container combinations for its cascading, waterfall form.

*R*ich in color and texture, H. Rhino Hide dances alongside Geranium Dark Reiter, a bi-color Bidens in red and yellow, Vertigo grass *(Pennisetum)* and a beautiful orange coleus splashed with berry red.

Design by Rob Zimmer

Design by Rob Zimmer

Flashes of purple on the underside of the leaves of this beautiful upright fuchsia and salmon superbells *(Calibrachoa)* greet H. Captain Kirk in this elegant cobalt pedestal bowl.

$\mathcal{S}$oothing, deep purple calla lilies and coral bell *(Heuchera)* add richness and beauty in this trio with H. Abiqua Drinking Gourd.

Design by Rob Zimmer

Color blast! H. Guardian Angel contrasts wonderfully with the rich two-tone reds of Fireworks Fountain Grass *(Pennisetum)* and a bright and bold coleus in lime and maroon.

Design by Rob Zimmer

Design by Rob Zimmer

Design by Rob Zimmer

Sharply designed, H. Diamonds Are Forever displays nicely beside a sparkling mass of Diamond Frost *(Euphorbia)*, black foliaged sweet potato vine *(Ipomoea)* and a burst of neon lantana *(Lantana)* that provides color and contrast to the cobalt container.

Design by Rob Zimmer

In this breathtaking container planting, H. Rhino Hide and H. Wave Runner are the perfect partners for the feathery texture of Japanese Painted Fern and cascading Creeping Jenny. The perfect container completes the look.

Design by Tammy Borden

Design by Tammy Borden

Design by Tammy Borden

One of my new favorite container plants is this beautiful Black Mondo Grass (*Ophiopogon*), a nice, compact dwarf, grass in deep black, joining lime green miniature H. Appletini and a splash of super bells (*Calibrachoa*) in pale pink.

Design by Rob Zimmer

In a towering blue container, the delicious, chocolate blades of Vertigo grass dance in flight over the fantastic, rippled foliage of white-rimmed H. Whee. Simply breathtaking.

Design by Rob Zimmer

Design by Rob Zimmer

ostas Joyride and Appletini make quite an impact in this gorgeous container planting that is full of color and motion. Salvia in apricot, a dramatic coleus in lime and strawberry and Concord Blue Streptocarpella round out the joyous combination.

Who needs blooms? I'm loving this icy combination of Icicles Licorice Plant, Fiber Optic Grass (*Isolepsis*) and, of course, H. Blue Mouse Ears.

Design by Rob Zimmer

Design by Rob Zimmer

$\mathscr{A}$gleaming, oval container large enough to hold giant H. Sum and Substance in brilliant lime, also boasts the four-season beauty of Purple Fountain Grass (*Pennisetum*) and a toothy, lime coleus with blood red stems.

*H*osta The King towers over this stunning dwarf trailing coleus in a vintage Redwing crock.

Design by Tammy Borden

Design by Tammy Borden

This eye-catching combination, adorning a large, silver container, features Fireworks Fountain Grass, variegated geranium and the powdery blue beauty of H. Kiwi Full Monty.

Design by Rob Zimmer

*I*n bold cobalt blue, this simple pairing of H. Praying Hands and Creeping Jenny in gorgeous lime green is captivating.

Design by Rob Zimmer

Design by Rob Zimmer

Design by Rob Zimmer

A young H. Victory makes a beautiful, if only temporary, specimen in this container featuring deep purple coleus and lime Creeping Jenny.

Design by Rob Zimmer

ℋosta Designer Genes has beautiful red stems or "legs" that complement Fireworks Fountain Grass and this beautiful coral bell in mauve, with an under planting of cascading Creeping Jenny.

Design by Sally Marchel Handrich

$\mathcal{N}$ative Prairie Dropseed (*Sporobolus*) is an unexpected delight in this simple, yet elegant planter featuring a sprawling specimen of H. Climax.

*J*une in spectacular prime, forms the centerpiece of this sprawling combination container that also features Japanese Forest Grass All Gold (*Hakonechloa*) and coleus in lime and rich purple.

Courtesy of Conny Parsons

Minis Divine

Courtesy of Conny Parsons

Courtesy of Conny Parsons

Whimsical and charming, this vintage bathtub is the perfect vessel for a trio of assorted hostas.

Courtesy of Conny Parsons

A beautiful combination of pink and gold lantana, Icicles Licorice Plant, Creeping Jenny and H. Rhino Hide.

Design by Rob Zimmer

Design by Rob Zimmer

This combination features H. Blue Mouse Ears, Fiber Optic Grass, a gorgeous copper coleus and glowing neon Creeping Jenny.

Purple and lime are a popular garden color combination for good reason. You cannot fail when it comes to combining plants in these wonderful hues. Here, H. Stained Glass, Japanese painted fern, Kong coleus and a variegated sedge share a dance.

Design by Rob Zimmer

$\mathcal{P}$urple Fountain grass waltzes gracefully above H. Guardian Angel and trailing Wandering Jew.

Design by Rob Zimmer

Design by Rob Zimmer

One of my favorite creations from this past summer, H. Whee is a centerpiece in this container featuring Vertigo grass *(Pennisetum)*, nemesia *(Nemesia)* in violet and rich purple super bells *(Calibrachoa)*.

DANCING IN THE WIND

Breathtaking hosta creations in flight

*D*ancing in the wind.

Over the past few growing seasons, I have explored the joys of growing hostas in hanging baskets. I first saw this demonstrated in the breathtaking hanging hosta gardens of Lindford, Hampshire, United Kingdom. Since those visions captivated my curiosity, I've recently begun diving into the world of hanging hostas in my own garden.

What a satisfying and rewarding journey it has been! Hosta lovers and non-hosta lovers alike swoon over the container plantings I have created over the past few seasons, whether presented as single specimen containers or in combination with annuals, even perennials, all in hanging baskets, perfect for displaying throughout the garden.

I've experimented using a number of different soils. I've attempted using soil containing moisture control crystals and not and I have seen no noticeable difference as far as the quality of the hostas in the container. A good quality potting mix is all that is needed.

As when creating hanging basket designs in general, it is nice to include several plant types to complete the look – a thriller, a spiller and a filler. The thriller is your centerpiece plant, which may or not be your hosta specimen. A filler is used to fill out the bulk of the container. Often, this may be a mounding, flowering annual with profuse blooms. It may also be a foliage plant, such as a coleus, a fern or a hosta. The spiller is used to create an elegant trailing or flowing cascade of foliage and bloom that drapes or sprawls from the edge of the basket.

Whether growing hanging baskets containing hostas in sun or shade, set a few of your favorite varieties free to dance with the wind.

Design by Rob Zimmer

*A*n elegant and unexpected combination of H. Blue Mouse Ears, variegated thyme, wire vine, Streptocarpella, Icicles licorice plant and Diamond Frost *(Euphorbia.)*

As this container fills out over spring and summer, the beautiful trailing form of Sweet Caroline sweet potato vine, wine and white nemesia and the eye catching beauty of H. Autumn Frost will create a treasured hanging hosta combination.

Design by Rob Zimmer

Design by Rob Zimmer

Hosta Joyride is set to dance in the wind with variegated vinca, Joseph's Coat (*Alternanthera*), a feathery red coleus, begonia and nemesia in beautiful blue.

$\mathscr{M}$exican Heather *(Cuphea)*, Creeping Jenny *(Lysimachia)*, Lotus vine *(Lotus)* in sea foam green, and H. Kiwi Full Monty.

Design by Rob Zimmer

$\mathcal{T}$he explosive blooms of these terra cotta super bells, along with variegated spike in chocolate and mint green, feathery coleus and plecanthrus in silver and purple ring H. Rhino Hide splendidly.

Design by Rob Zimmer

$\mathcal{V}$ariegated plecanthrus cascades from the edge of this hanging creation that features H. Guacamole in bright green with contrasting purple petunia that will fill out nicely over the summer season.

Design by Rob Zimmer

Super bells in two-toned pink and another in violet, lantana in bright orange, spreading licorice plant and H. June in early season splendor create a colorful and vibrant combination.

Design by Rob Zimmer

*I*mpatiens in hot pink, begonias in red and mauve sweet potato vine share the hosta dance with H. Diamonds Are Forever.

Design by Rob Zimmer

*W*himsical H. Whee commands attention in hanging baskets no matter what you choose to pair it with for the three-season dance.

Design by Rob Zimmer

The Art of Kokedama

Hosta Mighty Mouse makes the perfect, compact choice for this twine wrapped, moss laden Kokedama planter. A new trend now expanding throughout gardening circles, you'll discover a whole new way to grow hostas, as well as other perennials, annuals, succulents and house plants.

Design by Diane Van Horn

Design by Diane Van Horn

Made in the USA
Coppell, TX
17 June 2023